Workboo

MW00892594

Outlive

The Science & Art of Longevity

A Guide To Dr. Peter Attia's Book

Companion Press

Free Gift

As a thank you for your purchase, we are gifting you

five of our best selling, interactive workbooks for free.

To claim your gifts,

please scan the QR code below.

Note to Readers

This is an unofficial summary and analysis companion workbook based on *Outlive* by *Dr. Peter Attia*.

To purchase the original book,

please scan the QR code below.

Table of Contents

About "Outlive"

This book delves into the strategies and tactics that can not only extend your lifespan but also enhance your overall well-being. With a blend of personal anecdotes and thorough scientific studies, it delves into methods for averting age-related illnesses and maximizing the chances of a longer life.

The book emphasizes four key areas: Exercise, Nutrition, Sleep, and Emotional Health. It provides insights on utilizing these four pillars to optimize your health and steer clear of the "Four Horsemen" of chronic diseases—heart disease, cancer, Alzheimer's, and Type 2 diabetes.

Outlive empowers you by presenting actionable steps to prevent age-related decline. By the time you reach the conclusion of this book, you will possess a solid understanding of how to optimize your health and surpass your life expectancy.

Chapter 1: The Long Game

There are two distinct forms of death: swift and gradual. Swift deaths are often sudden and violent, such as those resulting from gunshots or car accidents. Gradual deaths, on the other hand, stem from chronic diseases that slowly erode one's vitality. Among these chronic diseases, age-related ailments like heart disease, Alzheimer's, cancer, and type 2 diabetes are the most prevalent and are commonly referred to as the "Four Horsemen."

Conventional medicine excels in addressing fast deaths through surgical interventions but falls short in comprehending and treating the underlying causes of slow deaths. Thus, a shift in our approach is necessary if we wish to prevent or postpone chronic diseases and enhance our longevity.

However, longevity encompasses more than just the number of years lived. It also encompasses the quality of health experienced as one ages, known as "healthspan." Merely reaching the age of 120 becomes meaningless if one is plagued by illness, frailty, and an inability to relish life. Therefore, it becomes crucial to discover methods of maintaining and improving our current state of health.

Key Points

- Conventional medicine treats trauma and chronic disease patients similarly, which is problematic for conditions like cancer and Alzheimer's.

- Despite significant investments in the War on Cancer, the mortality rate remains unchanged after 50 years

- A proactive approach is needed to combat slow death, focusing on treating chronic diseases before they become entrenched.

- Medical interventions should aim to address chronic diseases at an early stage rather than reacting after significant damage has occurred.

Healthspan Reflection Questions

Instructions: Set two personal health goals for yourself that align with the concept of "healthspan." In the space below, write down your goals and briefly explain why each goal is important to you. Consider aspects such as physical health, mental well-being, social connections, and personal fulfillment.

Goal:

_____

Explanation:

:_____

_____

Goal:

_____

Explanation:

:_____

_____

Mind Map to Health

In the space provided below the mind map, you can brainstorm different strategies, habits, and activities that can contribute to maintaining and improving your current state of health. Be creative and think beyond the conventional approaches. Add as many branches and sub-branches as you can.

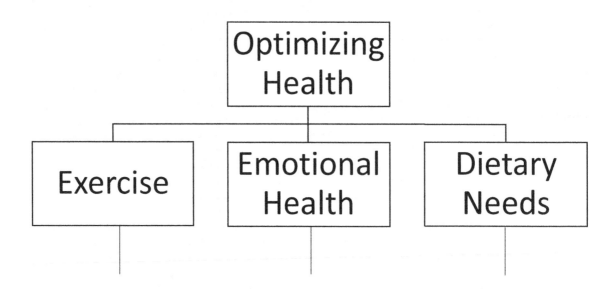

Longevity Role Models

In the space below, think of a person (real or fictional) who embodies the concept of living a long and healthy life. In the space below, describe this individual's characteristics, habits, and mindset that contribute to their longevity. Reflect on what you can learn from their example and how you can incorporate those elements into your own life.

My person is:		
Traits	**Hobbies**	**Mindset**

What can you do to fully embody this person in order to live a full, long, and healthy life?

_____

_____

_____

_____

_____

_____

Reflection Questions

Reflect on the difference between swift and gradual deaths. In the space below, write down your thoughts on these two distinct forms of death. How do they differ in their impact on individuals and their loved ones? How might these different forms of death influence our perspectives on life and health?

_____

_____

_____

Do you feel that the current healthcare system is fully serving patients' needs? Why or why not, and are you personally bias toward either answer?

_____

_____

_____

Write a short essay discussing the connection between emotional well-being and longevity. Explain how emotional factors such as stress, happiness, and social connections can impact healthspan. Share personal experiences or examples from research to support your points.

_____

_____

_____

Chapter 2: Medicine 3.0

One of the prominent hindrances in the progress of modern medicine lies in the resistance towards embracing innovation. The medical profession exhibits a risk-averse nature, displaying reluctance to adopt changes that challenge long-established traditions. Physicians tend to prioritize the principle of "doing no harm" over exploring radical and groundbreaking approaches to patient care.

This mentality harkens back to an outdated era of medical practice. The initial phase of medicine, known as Medicine 1.0, emerged thousands of years ago and relied primarily on conjecture rather than scientific knowledge. The subsequent era, Medicine 2.0, commenced in the mid-19th century and continues to this day, marked by advancements such as the invention of the microscope and the utilization of antimicrobial drugs.

However, it is imperative that we transition to Medicine 3.0, wherein the focus shifts towards disease prevention rather than merely providing pharmaceutical interventions once individuals have already fallen ill. Instead of solely resorting to surgical tumor removal, let us strive to assist patients in completely avoiding cancer. The necessary technological advancements are already at our disposal; all that remains is a transformative shift in mindset.

Key Points

- Medicine 3.0 emphasizes the study and prevention rather than the treatment of chronic diseases.

- Medicine 3.0 treats each patient as a unique person. Instead of treating every patient the same way, physicians can modify treatment to fit your unique physiology.

- In Medicine 3.0, doctors assess the risks and rewards of a particular treatment. If the risks outweigh the benefits to the patient, they may even decide not to treat the patient.

- Whereas Medicine 2.0 only focuses on increasing your lifespan, Medicine 3.0 emphasizes both lifespan and quality of life.

- Insurance companies don't pay doctors who advise patients to exercise or eat better. But they reimburse doctors who prescribe expensive drugs to sick patients.

- In Medicine 2.0, the patient is a helpless victim. In Medicine 3.0, the patient is expected to actively participate in determining their best treatment.

Innovations in Modern Medicine

Research and identify three recent innovations or advancements in the field of medicine. Describe each innovation and its potential impact on patient care. Discuss why these innovations are considered groundbreaking and how they challenge traditional approaches in the medical profession.

Innovation	Impact on society	Why is this groundbreaking?

Embracing Preventative Medicine

Below, write persuasive reasoning advocating for the transition to Medicine 3.0, with a focus on disease prevention. Explain why disease prevention should be prioritized over reactive interventions. Discuss the potential benefits of adopting a preventive approach to patient care and the role of technology in facilitating this shift.

_____

_____

_____

_____

_____

_____

_____

_____

_____

_____

_____

_____

_____

_____

_____

_____

_____

_____

_____

Comparative Analysis

Use the table below to compare the key characteristics and practices of Medicine 1.0, Medicine 2.0, and Medicine 3.0. Included in the columns are treatment, technological advancements, mindset, and prevention. Fill in the table with relevant information to highlight the differences between the three medical eras.

Medicine	Treatment	Tech Advancements	Mindset	Prevention
Medicine 1.0				
Medicine 2.0				
Medicine 3.0				

Reflection Questions

Do you feel the current healthcare system fully meets patients' needs? Explain your perspective, considering factors such as accessibility, affordability, quality of care, patient empowerment, and patient outcomes. Additionally, share your thoughts on the likelihood of future changes.

_____

_____

_____

The current healthcare system is more profit-oriented rather than patient-oriented. In light of this, reflect on the systemic factors contributing to this issue and propose concrete steps that can be taken to transform the healthcare system into a more patient-oriented approach. Consider the perspectives of different stakeholders, potential barriers to change, and innovative strategies that can prioritize patient well-being while ensuring sustainable healthcare delivery. Additionally, reflect on your own role as an individual and how you can contribute to the transformation.

_____

_____

_____

How can we collectively shift the mindset in medical schools from primarily treating disease to emphasizing disease prevention? Consider the factors influencing this mindset and propose practical steps that can be taken by medical institutions, policymakers, and society.

_____

_____

_____

Chapter 3: Objective, Strategy, Tactic

The common perception of longevity often revolves around envisioning elderly individuals grappling with cognitive decline and physical limitations. This stems from the fact that many people experience their later decades burdened by chronic diseases and restricted capabilities, leading us to accept the notion that enjoyment and vitality are elusive during this stage of life.

However, such thinking is misguided. It is indeed possible to envision the activities and experiences you desire during your later years and then devise the necessary strategies and tactics to help you achieve them. To do so, it becomes imperative to enhance both your physical and cognitive functions as you age.

There are no shortcuts in this process. If your goal is to improve both your lifespan and healthspan, it is crucial to develop strategies that align with this objective. Subsequently, these overarching strategies can be broken down into specific tactics that you can implement on a daily basis, ensuring steady progress towards your desired outcomes.

Key Points

- The most straightforward way to attain longevity is to avoid the Four Horsemen of chronic disease—cancer, heart disease, Alzheimer's, and type 2 diabetes.

- Without a clear understanding of your strategy, your tactics will be ineffective. You'll end up relying on Medicine 2.0—seeking a shortcut to your health problems.

- As you age, your quality of health is determined by the deterioration of three vectors: cognitive, physical, and emotional function. You need to maintain all three vectors.

- When you improve your healthspan, you automatically improve your lifespan. Therefore, focus your tactics on enhancing your healthspan.

- Medicine 3.0 incorporates five main tactics for improving healthspan: Exercise, Nutrition, Sleep, Emotional health, and Supplements.

- Make sure that your tactics are constantly evolving as you move through life.

Cognitive Stimulation Activities

Compile a list of cognitive stimulation activities that you find enjoyable and engaging. This can include reading challenging books, solving puzzles, learning a new language, playing musical instruments, or engaging in strategic games. Create a schedule or weekly planner to incorporate these activities into your routine, ensuring a well-rounded cognitive workout.

Activity	Day of Week	Notes

Social Connections Inventory

Conduct an inventory of your social connections and evaluate their impact on your well-being. Create a table with columns for the names of individuals, the nature of the relationship, and the level of support and connection you feel from each person. Reflect on the quality and quantity of your social connections, and identify areas for improvement or expansion.

Name	Relationship	Connection/Support	Improvements?

Physical Fitness Plan

Develop a personalized physical fitness plan that aligns with your longevity goals. Include a combination of cardiovascular exercises, strength training, flexibility work, and balance activities. Set specific goals, such as the number of workouts per week and the duration of each session. Use a table or checklist to track your progress and celebrate milestones achieved along the way.

Exercise	Workouts per week	Duration

Reflection Questions

Have you developed a proactive plan to delay cognitive and physical decline as you age, considering activities for cognitive stimulation, physical exercise, nutrition, stress management, social engagement, and preventive healthcare? Reflect on your plan and assess its effectiveness.

_____

_____

_____

How can you incorporate more exercise into your daily routine in ways that bring you joy and align with your interests? Reflect on creative strategies, such as finding enjoyable activities, leveraging social connections, utilizing outdoor environments, and managing your time effectively. Embrace experimentation and exploration to discover a fulfilling exercise routine.

_____

_____

_____

Consider your understanding of longevity. Has it been influenced by perceptions of age and illness? How might changing your perspective about aging influence your approach to your healthspan and lifespan?

_____

_____

_____

Chapter 4: Centenarians

The quest to unravel the secrets behind the remarkable longevity of centenarians captivates us all. Is it a stroke of luck, their genetic makeup, or perhaps their unconventional lifestyles? Discovering the answers to these questions holds the promise of adopting certain daily rituals that could potentially enhance our own lifespans. This pursuit is of great significance because centenarians defy the aging process experienced by the average individual.

A notable distinction lies in the fact that centenarians tend to develop chronic diseases much later in life compared to the general population. For instance, while the average person may receive a cancer diagnosis by the age of 72, centenarians typically experience such ailments only after reaching the remarkable milestone of 100 years. In essence, centenarians possess the ability to extend their period of robust health long after others have succumbed to chronic diseases.

By unraveling the factors contributing to their prolonged well-being, we can aspire to enhance our own quality of life and potentially postpone the onset of age-related illnesses.

Key Points

- Genes are responsible for 20-30 percent of your lifespan. For example, you're more likely to be a centenarian if your sibling lived beyond 100.

- There are four times more female than male centenarians.

- Male centenarians are more cognitively and physically healthy than their female counterparts.

- Most centenarians spend their entire lives healthier and biologically younger than their peers. For example, at 60, a centenarian can have the coronary arteries of a 35-year-old.

- Living to be 100 and beyond is all about making small interventions that cumulatively improve your health.

- Becoming a centenarian depends on how resilient you are. It comes down to your ability to resist chronic disease—even if you smoke, drink alcohol, or have a poor diet.

Centenarian Interviews

Research stories and interviews of centenarians who have defied the aging process and maintained vibrant health. Use the document below to analyze their daily rituals, habits, and lifestyle choices. Look for common patterns and identify specific practices that stand out to you as potential contributors to their prolonged well-being.

Name	Daily habits/rituals	Lifestyle choices	Can you implement?

Longevity Lifestyle Assessment

Evaluate your current lifestyle and identify areas where you can make positive changes to support longevity. Deeply consider all factors, like social interactions with friends and physical activity during the day.

Factors	Satisfaction on 1-10 scale	What do you like?	What don't you like?	How can you improve?
Emotional				
Physical				
Dietary				
Social				

Longevity Action Plan

Develop a comprehensive action plan for promoting longevity in your life. Use the table below to outline specific goals, strategies, and action steps related to nutrition, exercise, sleep, stress management, cognitive engagement, and social connections. Regularly review and update your action plan, celebrating milestones and adjusting strategies as needed to ensure continuous progress towards your desired outcomes.

Activity	Goal	Check in

Reflection Questions

Consider the role of genetics in longevity. How does the idea that centenarians have unique genetic advantages impact your own beliefs about aging and the potential for extending your lifespan? How can you strike a balance between acknowledging genetic predispositions and embracing lifestyle choices that influence your overall well-being?

_____

_____

_____

Reflect on your own fears or concerns related to aging and longevity. What specific worries or anxieties arise when contemplating the aging process? How can you reframe these concerns and cultivate a more positive and empowered mindset that focuses on proactive measures for healthy aging?

_____

_____

_____

Reflect on the importance of purpose and meaning in the context of aging and longevity. How does having a sense of purpose and engaging in meaningful activities contribute to healthy aging and overall well-being? How can you cultivate and nurture a sense of purpose in your own life?

_____

_____

_____

Chapter 5: Eat Less, Live Longer

Initially recognized for its antimicrobial properties, rapamycin is a natural compound that has since unveiled a plethora of distinctive attributes and medical applications. One of its most notable characteristics lies in its profound influence on cell division and growth. But how does this relate to longevity?

Rapamycin exerts its effects directly on an intracellular protein called mTOR (mechanistic target of rapamycin). This ubiquitous protein, present in all life forms, plays a pivotal role in determining the lifespan of your cells. When you consume an abundance of food, rapamycin activates mTOR, triggering cell growth and division. This process consumes substantial energy and ultimately diminishes your lifespan.

Conversely, when you restrict your nutrient intake, rapamycin inhibits mTOR. As a result, your body halts the process of cell growth and instead begins recycling older cells. This cellular cleanup process holds the potential to bolster your overall lifespan. Hence, it appears that reducing calorie consumption may be linked to an extended life expectancy.

By understanding the intricate interplay between rapamycin, mTOR, and cellular processes, we gain insights into the fascinating relationship between nutrient intake, cell growth, and longevity.

Key Points

- The concept of eating less to live longer is not new. It goes back centuries, all the way back to Hippocrates.

- Caloric restriction means controlling the calories you consume while still taking in the necessary nutrients.

- Caloric restriction increases lifespan, metabolic efficiency, cellular stress resistance, and the production of new mitochondria.

- Consuming fewer calories stimulates autophagy—the process where old and weak cells are broken down into amino acids to create new cells.

- Autophagy is so vital that if it were to shut down, the organism would become diseased and die.

- Other than fasting, you can stimulate autophagy through exercise.

- Though caloric restriction is beneficial, it has its drawbacks. Very lean animals may be at risk of death from cold temperatures or infection. Long-term calorie restriction is also not sustainable for most people.

Cellular Rejuvenation Visualization

Engage in a guided visualization exercise focused on cellular rejuvenation. Close your eyes and imagine your cells undergoing a rejuvenating process, renewing and optimizing their functions. Visualize the inhibitory effects of rapamycin on mTOR, promoting cellular cleanup and longevity. Journal your experience and note any shifts in your mindset or motivation towards supporting cellular health.

_____

_____

_____

_____

_____

_____

_____

_____

_____

_____

_____

_____

_____

_____

_____

_____

_____

_____

_____

Weekly Fasting Protocol

Explore the practice of intermittent fasting as a strategy to modulate mTOR activity and promote longevity. Design a fasting protocol that suits your lifestyle, such as a 16:8 (16 hours of fasting, 8 hours of eating) or 5:2 (five days of regular eating, two days of restricted calories) approach. Monitor your fasting days and document your observations and feelings throughout the process.

(Note: This is not medical advise. Make sure to speak with a licensed clinician before undergoing any type of fast.)

Fast type	Day(s) of week	Positive/negative notes

Longevity Legends Interview

Imagine you have the opportunity to interview a centenarian who has defied the aging process. Create a list of intriguing questions you would ask them about their lifestyle, mindset, and daily routines. Truly try to embody this person, then write down their hypothetical responses and reflect on the wisdom and insights gained from this imaginary conversation.

Name:

_____

Questions you'd ask:

_____

_____

_____

_____

_____

Hypothetical answers:

_____

_____

_____

_____

_____

_____

_____

_____

_____

_____

Reflection Questions

Describe the longest period during which you willingly abstained from consuming any food and reflect upon the impact it had on your physical, mental, and emotional well-being. Consider the changes you experienced in terms of energy levels, focus, mood, and overall health.

_____

_____

_____

How does the mechanism connecting caloric restriction and longevity operate at the cellular and molecular level? Explore the activation of key signaling pathways, such as mTOR and AMPK, and their effects on cellular metabolism, stress response, and aging. Consider the impact on factors like DNA repair, inflammation, oxidative stress, and mitochondrial function, and reflect on how this understanding can inform strategies for promoting longevity through dietary interventions.

_____

_____

_____

What are the potential drawbacks of implementing caloric restriction in your life? Consider factors such as the risk of nutrient deficiencies, impacts on social interactions and enjoyment of food, and potential psychological and emotional effects. How can you adjust to make it work for your lifestyle?

_____

_____

_____

Chapter 6: The Crisis of Abundance

During our ancestral hunter-gatherer era, prolonged periods of famine were commonplace. As a survival mechanism, our genetic makeup evolved to efficiently convert calories into fatty tissue, serving as a crucial energy reserve during times of scarcity. However, with the advent of technology, we now have unrestricted access to a wide variety of food options. Unfortunately, our genetic predisposition to convert calories into fat remains unchanged.

Compounding this issue is the excessive presence of sugar, particularly fructose, in our modern diet. Fructose is abundantly found in numerous food products we consume daily, ranging from salad dressings to pastries. When consumed in excess, fructose is rapidly stored as fat in the liver, leading to the accumulation of fatty tissue and subsequent metabolic dysfunction.

Metabolic dysfunction serves as the underlying precursor for many chronic diseases we encounter today. It is noteworthy that a significant proportion of individuals exhibit metabolic unhealthiness despite not yet presenting any of the commonly recognized chronic diseases prevalent in our modern society. Consequently, it becomes crucial to address the fundamental problem of metabolic dysfunction as a priority, rather than fixating solely on specific diseases such as obesity.

Key Points

- When excess fat is stored or produced in the liver, it creates a condition known as nonalcoholic fatty liver disease (NAFLD).

- NAFLD leads to liver inflammation—a condition known as nonalcoholic steatohepatitis (NASH). Unfortunately, the early stages of NAFLD and NASH have no symptoms and cannot be picked up in a blood test.

- NAFLD is highly correlated to obesity. If a patient loses weight, then they can reverse NAFLD and NASH.

- The liver is the most resilient and regenerative organ in your body. It can recover from practically any kind of damage.

- A lot of focus is placed on the obesity problem yet obesity is just a symptom of metabolic dysfunction. We need to focus on metabolic health more than anything else.

- Some people are obese yet metabolically healthy, while others can be metabolically unhealthy yet not obese.

- Metabolic dysfunction is defined by five criteria: *High blood pressure, low HDL cholesterol, high triglycerides, elevated fasting glucose, and large waist circumference.*

Sugar Detox Challenge

Challenge yourself to a week-long sugar detox by eliminating added sugars and high-fructose foods from your diet. Keep a journal to record your experiences, including any changes in cravings, energy levels, and overall well-being.

Date	Cravings 1-10	Energy 1-10	Well-being 1-10	Notes

Mindful Eating Reflection

Take a moment to reflect on your eating habits and cultivate mindfulness around your meals. Set aside dedicated time for a meal and follow these steps:

Preparing the Environment: Create a calm and inviting space for your meal. Set the table, eliminate distractions, and choose pleasant lighting and soothing background music if desired. How does your space feel now, as opposed to it usually feels when you're about to eat?

_____

_____

_____

Engage Your Senses: Before taking your first bite, take a few deep breaths to center yourself. Observe the visual appeal of your food, noticing its colors, shapes, and textures. Pay attention to the aromas wafting from your plate. What do you notice visually within this meal that you usually don't?

_____

_____

_____

Mindful Bites: Take your first bite slowly and deliberately. Notice the flavors as they unfold on your tongue. Chew each bite thoroughly, savoring the taste and texture. Put down your utensils between bites to fully experience the present moment. What does it taste like as compared to a "normal" meal?

_____

_____

_____

Mindful Eating Reflection (Continued)

Physical Cues: Tune in to your body's signals of hunger and fullness. Pause periodically during the meal and check in with yourself. Are you still hungry? Are you starting to feel satisfied? Pay attention to these cues and eat until you feel comfortably satiated. What is your body telling you?

_____

_____

_____

Emotional Awareness: Observe any emotions or thoughts that arise during your meal. Are you eating out of genuine hunger or in response to stress, boredom, or other triggers? Acknowledge these emotions without judgment and explore alternative ways to address them. Are you experiencing any emotional responses? Explore them below.

_____

_____

_____

Gratitude Practice: Cultivate a sense of gratitude for the food you are consuming. Reflect on the journey it took for the ingredients to reach your plate, from the farmers who grew the produce to the hands that prepared the meal. Express gratitude for nourishing your body and supporting your well-being. Does your gratitude for the food change your experience? Why or why not?

_____

_____

_____

Healthy Snack Ideas

It is important to maintaining a nutritious diet includes making smart choices even when it comes to snacking. Below is a table of healthy snacks that you can pick and choose from. Circle each of these you have a taste for, and make it a point to set them aside for when you're feeling hungry.

Snack Ideas	Description
Fresh fruits	Apples, oranges, berries
Raw nuts/seeds	Almonds, walnuts, pumpkin seeds
Greek yogurt/cottage cheese	Pair with fruits, nuts, or a drizzle of honey
Vegetable sticks	Carrot, celery, bell pepper with hummus, guacamole, or yogurt dip
Air-popped popcorn	Homemade kale chips
Hard-boiled eggs	Enjoy on their own or with whole grain crackers or sliced veggies
Dried fruits	Raisins, apricots, dried cranberries
Rice cakes/whole grain crackers	Topped with avocado, tomato slices, or lean protein like turkey or chicken breast
Homemade smoothies	Fruits, leafy greens, and protein source like Greek yogurt or plant-based protein powder
Dark chocolate	70% cocoa or higher, a small portion with potential health benefits

Pick, choose, and add to the list above. Which ones are your favorite?

_____

Reflection Questions

The statement that obesity is a symptom rather than the core issue can be a radical shift in perspective. Reflect on how this shift affects your perception of your health or societal health as a whole. How does this impact your attitude toward weight management and overall wellness?

_____

_____

_____

With the understanding that metabolic dysfunction is the hidden culprit behind many chronic diseases, reflect on your health journey. How has your lifestyle possibly influenced your metabolic health over the years? How does this newfound knowledge change the lens through which you view your health, and what conscious decisions are you considering to enhance your metabolic health?

_____

_____

_____

The liver's remarkable ability to heal and regenerate itself presents a powerful opportunity for health restoration. With this knowledge in mind, how does this influence your commitment to liver health? How might you adapt your current lifestyle habits to support this incredible organ in its essential work?

_____

_____

_____

Chapter 7: The Ticker

Heart disease and stroke stand as the primary global causes of death, surpassing even cancer. In the United States alone, approximately 2,300 individuals succumb to atherosclerotic cardiovascular disease each day. Paradoxically, despite its staggering impact, heart disease often receives less awareness and attention compared to cancer. Consequently, it appears that we are silently losing the battle against this world's deadliest killer.

However, this dire situation can be altered. Preventing heart disease is comparatively easier than both cancer and Alzheimer's, and while it may not be reversible, its onset can be delayed through early detection. The challenge lies in our limited understanding of its root causes and development.

The issue with the prevailing Medicine 2.0 approach is that it primarily intervenes when heart disease has already reached an advanced stage. To overcome this, we must adopt a strategy that addresses the risks associated with all forms of atherosclerotic cardiovascular disease, aiming to eliminate the threat of fatal outcomes by implementing timely and appropriate measures.

Key Points

- Apart from transporting oxygen and nutrients, your blood also carries cholesterol—an essential element for producing hormones, acids, and membranes.

- A major misconception is that cholesterol from diet causes heart disease. Most of the cholesterol in your blood actually comes from your cells. Therefore, you don't have to be concerned about overconsuming cholesterol.

- Heart disease can also affect young people. 50 percent of cardiovascular problems occur in people under the age of 65.

- Atherosclerosis is slow and sneaky, which means it can develop while you're a teenager and only become problematic when you're much older.

- Smoking and high blood pressure are two major risk factors for cardiovascular disease.

- Nearly every adult has some vascular damage. Though most doctors aren't concerned by this, it's important to take action that delays further damage to your heart muscles.

Lifestyle Habit Tracker

In this table, you can track key lifestyle habits that impact heart health on a daily basis. Here's how to use it: physical Activity (minutes): Write down the number of minutes you spent engaging in physical activity each day, such as walking, jogging, cycling, or participating in a workout session. Smoking (number of cigarettes): If you smoke, record the number of cigarettes you smoked on each day. If you don't smoke, you can leave this column blank. Alcohol Consumption (units): Note the number of alcohol units you consumed each day. Keep in mind the recommended limits for moderate alcohol consumption (e.g., 1 drink per day for women, 2 drinks per day for men). Stress Management Technique: Write down the stress management technique you practiced on each day. It could be meditation, deep breathing exercises, journaling, or any other technique that helps you reduce stress levels.

By regularly updating this lifestyle habit tracker, you can visually monitor your habits and identify patterns or areas for improvement.

Lifestyle Habit Tracker	Monday	Tuesday	Wednesday	Thursday	Friday	Saturday	Sunday
Physical Activity (minutes)							
Smoking (number of cigarettes)							
Alcohol Consumption (units)							
Stress Management Technique							

Inspirational Heart Healthy Stories

In this exercise, you will explore inspirational stories of individuals who have overcome heart disease or made significant improvements in their heart health. These stories serve as a source of motivation and inspiration, showing what is possible when it comes to preventing and managing heart disease. First, find an inspirational story, then evaluate how you can implement the information into your own life.

Steps they took to improve heart health and disease:

_____

_____

_____

How did this story make you feel?

_____

_____

_____

How can you implement this information into your daily life?

_____

_____

_____

Risk Assessment

In this interactive table, assess each risk factor by placing a checkmark in the appropriate box next to "Yes" or "No" to indicate whether the risk factor applies to you. Consider factors such as your family history, lifestyle choices, and overall health. This will help you identify areas of potential risk for heart disease. Once completed, you can review the table to gain insights into your individual risk profile and prioritize areas for improvement or further evaluation.

Remember to consult with a healthcare professional for a comprehensive assessment and personalized guidance based on your specific health situation.

Risk Factor	Yes	No
Family History		
High Blood Pressure		
High Cholesterol		
Smoking		
Diabetes		
Obesity		
Sedentary Lifestyle		
Poor Diet		
Stress		
Age		

Reflection Questions

Why do you think Medicine 2.0 has fallen short in adequately tackling the underlying factors contributing to the development and progression of heart disease? In your response, consider the prevailing approaches in Medicine 2.0 that primarily focus on interventions during advanced stages of the disease, rather than prioritizing early detection and preventive measures.

_____

_____

_____

In addition to the conventional methods of preventing and treating heart disease, what alternative approaches or therapies have shown promise in improving cardiovascular health and reducing the risk of heart disease? And which ones would you like to partake in?

_____

_____

_____

Smoking and high blood pressure are two major risk factors for cardiovascular disease. Reflect on your lifestyle and habits; are these two risk factors relevant to you? If so, what steps can you take to reduce these risks?

_____

_____

_____

Chapter 8: The Runaway Cell

Similar to heart disease, cancer prevalence grows exponentially as each decade passes. Since the declaration of the War on Cancer in 1971, immense amounts of funding have been allocated towards finding a cure. While progress has been made in treating specific types of cancer, such as leukemia and Hodgkin's lymphoma, overall mortality rates have remained unchanged.

The primary challenge in combating cancer lies in its ability to overwhelm the body, leaving few options for effective intervention once it has metastasized. While surgery, radiation, and chemotherapy can be effective, their efficacy diminishes significantly when dealing with advanced or metastatic tumors. Additionally, our medical systems often struggle with early detection, frequently identifying cancer only after it has spread extensively or reached an advanced stage where complete removal becomes challenging.

Confronted with these obstacles, a shift in strategy becomes imperative. Firstly, our focus should be on prevention, sparing no effort to minimize the occurrence of cancer. Though complex, prevention is attainable. Secondly, we must leverage innovative treatments that target the vulnerabilities of cancer cells, capitalizing on their weaknesses. Lastly, substantial investment in precise and reliable early detection methods is necessary to enhance the effectiveness of our treatments.

By adopting this multi-faceted approach, combining prevention, targeted treatments, and improved detection, we can forge a more promising path towards combating cancer and reducing its devastating impact.

Key Points

- Cancer cells are normal cells that don't stop growing. This is due to a genetic mutation in cells.

- Cancer cells can move from one organ to another, thus turning a localized problem into a deadly systemic disease.

- It's difficult to find a cancer cure because it's a random and complex condition. Each type of cancer has a different genetic sequence. Also, a breast cancer tumor in one patient can have a different genome from a similar tumor in another patient.

- Cancer cells that survive chemotherapy usually mutate and become stronger than before.

- Cancer cells have two unique traits: they consume a large amount of glucose and can easily evade the immune system.

- The leading risk factors for cancer are obesity and smoking.

- Calorie restriction lowers cancer risk and slows down the growth of cancers. Therefore, improving your metabolic health is an effective way to prevent cancer.

- The best way to beat cancer is to target all its vulnerabilities at the same time.

Lifestyle Changes Tracker

In this interactive tracker, take a moment to think about your goals for each lifestyle change. What specific actions can you take to make those changes a reality? Fill in the "Progress" column as you make progress, celebrate achievements, and note any challenges you face along the way.

Remember, this tracker is here to support and motivate you on your journey to a healthier lifestyle. Check back regularly.

Lifestyle Change	Goal	Action Steps	Progress
Healthy Eating			
Regular Exercise			
Stress Management			
Adequate Sleep			
Tobacco and Alcohol			
Screen Time Control			

Empathy and Compassion Exercise

Choose a specific cancer patient, caregiver, or healthcare professional whose perspective you would like to explore.. Write a short narrative that depicts their daily life, struggles, moments of hope, and acts of resilience. Now, imagine yourself stepping into their shoes and experiencing their journey firsthand. Reflect on the following questions and write down your responses:

How did it feel to inhabit their perspective and witness their challenges?

_____

_____

What emotions did you experience while imagining their journey?

_____

_____

What insights or new understanding did you gain about the human impact of cancer?

_____

_____

In what ways can you apply this newfound understanding and empathy in your interactions with others?

_____

_____

Reflection Questions

Reflecting on the chapter's insights about cancer treatment, contemplate the following question: What are the fundamental shifts in mindset and approach that need to occur in our society to revolutionize the way we approach and treat cancer?

_____

_____

_____

In what ways has this chapter challenged or shifted your understanding of the critical role that early detection and prevention play in the battle against cancer? Reflect on the specific information and insights presented, such as the limitations of advanced-stage treatments and the potential impact of timely interventions

_____

_____

_____

Reflect on the importance of empathy and compassion in supporting individuals affected by cancer. How can you cultivate these qualities in your interactions with others?

_____

_____

_____

Chapter 9: Chasing Memory

Among the Four Horsemen of chronic diseases, Alzheimer's remains the most enigmatic. While we have knowledge on preventing heart disease, the ability to detect and treat cancer, and even the potential to reverse type 2 diabetes, the origins and mechanisms of Alzheimer's disease continue to elude us.

Alzheimer's is characterized by the accumulation of brain plaques formed by a protein called amyloid-beta. Initially, this protein was considered the primary culprit behind Alzheimer's. However, emerging research has cast doubt on this theory. Despite numerous drug development efforts aimed at eliminating amyloid-beta, none have successfully treated Alzheimer's.

Neurodegenerative diseases, including Parkinson's and Lewy body dementia, present similar challenges to medical researchers. The lack of success in developing effective treatments has necessitated a shift towards preventive strategies as a potential solution.

In light of the ongoing uncertainties surrounding the causes and treatments of Alzheimer's and other neurodegenerative diseases, emphasis is being placed on exploring alternative avenues focused on prevention. By delving into preventive measures, we aim to confront the complex nature of these diseases and pave the way for potential breakthroughs in understanding, managing, and ultimately mitigating their impact.

Key Points

- Studies show that nutrition, exercise, and cognitive training can help prevent cognitive decline among the elderly.

- Alzheimer's is twice as prevalent in women than in men. This could be hormonal changes after menopause and the use of oral contraceptives.

- The most challenging part of diagnosing neurodegenerative diseases is interpreting test results to identify whether a patient is suffering from Alzheimer's, dementia, or Parkinson's.

- Alzheimer's and dementia patients somehow adapt to damage to their brains. This makes it difficult to diagnose the early stages of neurodegeneration.

- You can delay cognitive decline by enhancing your neural networks through education, speaking a foreign language, or learning to play an instrument.

- Complex movements and exercises such as boxing and dancing have proven to be most effective at preventing or delaying Parkinson's.

- Stroke victims are more susceptible to Alzheimer's due to the prior blockage of blood flow to the brain.

Digital Detox Exercise

Digital Detox Period _____

I will abstain from using _____ during my digital detox.

I will avoid accessing _____ or _____.

I will communicate my intentions with _____.

Alternative Activities:

_____

_____

_____

Digital-Free Environment:

I will turn off notifications on _____.

I will keep my devices out of sight and in _____.

I will create physical boundaries, such as _____.

Reflection:

During my digital detox, I noticed changes in my _____.

I discovered that without digital distractions, I had more time for _____.

I found it challenging to _____ without digital devices.

Insights and Learnings:

One insight I gained from the digital detox was _____.

I learned that I rely on digital devices for _____.

Moving forward, I plan to establish healthier digital habits by _____.

Mental Sharpening Activity

Discover and commit to learning new mental sharpening skills. This could include simple activities like a Rubiks Cube, mastering puzzles, memory enhancement, or even mindfulness techniques like meditation. Do research, choose three that excite you, then fill in the table below. Assess your improvement one month later.

Activity	Date	Assess Your First Time Doing This Activity	Assess Your Improvement

The Dancer's Mind

Dance is a universal language that speaks to both the body and the mind. It's more than just a form of exercise or artistic expression; it is also a cognitive challenge that engages multiple parts of the brain, providing a unique platform for the simultaneous enhancement of physical and cognitive health.

When you think of dancing, you probably think of rhythm, flexibility, and coordination, but dance also demands memory, attention, and quick decision-making. Reflect on this dual nature of dancing - how could incorporating this multi-layered activity into your routine potentially contribute to the improvement of your cognitive health?

_____

_____

_____

Dancing has physical benefits such as improved cardiovascular health, balance, and flexibility, but it also brings mental benefits like increased alertness, spatial awareness, and even emotional release. What do you imagine the mental and physical benefits of dancing would be?

_____

_____

_____

From the grace of a ballet dancer to the energy of a street dancer, every dance step we take has the potential to enhance not only our physical strength but also our cognitive resilience. With this exercise, it's hoped that you begin to see dance not just as an art or hobby, but as a unique partner in your journey toward cognitive health and longevity.

Reflection Questions

Studies underline the benefits of nutrition, exercise, and cognitive training in preventing cognitive decline. Personalize this to your current lifestyle - are there areas where you could improve? How might you incorporate these pillars of prevention more effectively into your daily routines?

_____

_____

_____

Parkinson's, another formidable neurodegenerative disease, has shown susceptibility to complex exercises like boxing and dancing. If you were to introduce these activities into your routine, how could you creatively integrate them? Imagine a week in your life with these exercises – what could that look like?

_____

_____

_____

Reflect on the impact of technology and digital devices on your cognitive well-being. How did the digital detox resonate with you? Assess the challenges you've faced, emotions you had, and overall well being during the detox period.

_____

_____

_____

Chapter 10: Thinking Tactically

The rapid rise in cancer rates correlates with the rapid industrialization and urbanization of society, surpassing the pace at which our genes can adapt. This trend underscores the need to find a balance between societal progress and maintaining our health. Rather than abandoning progress, our focus should be on developing strategies that enable us to adapt to this evolving world.

One crucial approach is to examine our environment and its detrimental effects on our well-being. By minimizing the negative impacts of our created environment, we can reduce the risk of premature death and enhance our overall quality of life. However, to maximize the effectiveness of these strategies, it is essential to concentrate on specific areas that have the most significant influence on our health.

Moreover, it is crucial to acknowledge the uniqueness of each individual. Recognizing that each person possesses distinct traits and health conditions, the application of tactics should be tailored to cater to their specific needs. Rather than prescribing a generic solution, doctors can guide patients in formulating individualized healthcare regimens that align with their personal characteristics.

By embracing this comprehensive and personalized approach, we can navigate the challenges posed by our modern environment while promoting longevity and improved well-being for individuals on a personalized level.

Key Points

- There are five key areas that you can address to increase your lifespan and healthspan: exercise, nutrition, sleep, emotional health, and pharmaceutical drugs.

- To generate the biggest impact on your health, focus on exercise and nutrition. Examine whether you have enough muscle mass and are consuming adequate calories.

- If you're overweight, don't just think about how to reduce your caloric intake.—also consider ways to gain more muscle.

- Developing good tactics for improving your health first requires you to recognize your key danger points. Only then can you create *specific, actionable* tactics. Your body will give you feedback on whether a tactic is working or not. If it's not, adjust accordingly.

- Your best option is to create a personalized playbook that suits your health needs rather than blindly copying what everyone else is doing. A generic prescription can only take you so far.

Environmental Audit Exercise

In this table, you can fill in the different environments you want to audit, such as your living space, workplace, commuting, outdoor spaces, personal care routine, etc. Under the "Potential Sources of Toxins/Pollutants" column, list specific items or activities that may introduce toxins or pollutants into that environment. In the "Solutions/Improvements" column, brainstorm and write down possible solutions or improvements to minimize the impact of those sources. This will help you identify areas where you can make changes to create a healthier environment.

Environment	Sources of Toxins	Solutions/Improvements
Living Space		
Workplace		
Commuting		
Outdoor Spaces		
Personal Care		
Cleaning Products		
Food and Beverages		
Electronic Devices		
Hobbies and Crafts		
Other (Specify)		

Design Your Healthy Environment

Imagine your ideal healthy environment. Draw a blueprint or create a visual representation of this environment, incorporating elements that promote well-being, such as green spaces, natural lighting, and clean air. Annotate your design with explanations of how each element contributes to your health. Create this representation below.

Nature Connection Journal

The Nature Connection Journal serves as a powerful tool for immersing ourselves in nature, promoting mindfulness, strengthening our bond with the natural world, and personalizing our well-being practices. It aligns with the chapter's message of finding balance in an evolving world and nurturing our health in the face of environmental challenges. Fill in each section, and be sure to be with nature at least once a week.

Location	Date/Tme	Observation	Feelings/Emotions

Reflection Questions

How can you integrate the principles and strategies discussed throughout this workbook into your daily life? What small, yet significant, changes can you make to align your habits, mindset, and lifestyle choices with the pursuit of a vibrant and fulfilling existence?

_____

_____

_____

Reflecting on your age, physical condition, lifestyle, and individual needs, contemplate the specific exercises that hold the potential to optimize your health and promote muscle growth. How can you customize your exercise routine to address your unique circumstances and maximize the benefits you desire?

_____

_____

_____

How can you optimize your self in a way that is catered to your surroundings and lifestyle? Consider factors such as creating a peaceful bedtime routine, optimizing your sleep environment, and incorporating relaxation techniques.

_____

_____

_____

Chapter 11: Exercise

The ongoing debate between weight training and cardio often overshadows the fact that any form of exercise brings significant benefits to the body. Exercise has been extensively researched and proven to offer numerous health advantages. Surprisingly, dedicating just 90 minutes per week to exercise can reduce the risk of mortality by 14 percent.

Despite the well-established benefits, the medical profession falls short in recommending exercise as a preventive and therapeutic measure for various diseases. Studies have consistently shown that exercise is as effective as, if not better than, pharmaceutical drugs in preventing death from conditions such as heart disease, stroke, and diabetes.

Moreover, natural muscle mass decline is a part of the aging process. Therefore, it becomes crucial to proactively work towards maintaining adequate muscle mass and cardiovascular fitness as the years progress. Age should never be a barrier to commencing an exercise routine. It is advisable to engage in a diverse range of exercises, akin to a decathlon athlete, to ensure a well-rounded fitness regimen.

By recognizing the immense value of exercise and integrating it into our lifestyles, we can harness its preventative and therapeutic potential, promoting long-term health and vitality regardless of age or specific exercise preference.

Key Points

- If there's one thing you should add to your life, it's exercise. Even a little bit of exercise can boost longevity, delay chronic disease, prevent physical decline, and even slow down cognitive damage.

- Exercise strengthens your heart, enhances the functioning of mitochondria, boosts your immune system, improves memory, and preserves brain volume.

- The single most powerful indicator of longevity is your peak aerobic fitness (VO_2 max). This is the maximum rate at which your body's muscles can use oxygen. A higher VO_2 max correlates to lower mortality.

- Having a below-average VO_2 max puts you at greater risk of death than smoking!

- Focus on building muscle strength and not just muscle mass. Your muscle's ability to generate force is what reduces your mortality risk.

- Instead of obsessing over one specific type of exercise, e.g. cycling, start incorporating diverse exercises in your workout regimen. For example, create a routine that includes swimming, walking, cycling, weightlifting, etc.

Fitness Myth Busting

In this exercise, you'll explore and debunk common fitness myths that may hinder your progress or understanding of exercise. Each row in the table presents a fitness myth, and your task is to fill in the blank with the corresponding truth. Do your research, and find common fitness myths that many people believe. By doing so, you'll gain a better understanding of the reality behind these misconceptions.

Myth	Truth
Lifting weights makes women bulky.	Weightlifting helps build lean muscle and improve overall strength without causing excessive bulkiness in women.
Cardio is the best way to burn fat.	While cardio is effective for burning calories, incorporating strength training into your routine can help increase muscle mass and boost metabolism for long-term fat loss.

Mind Body Connection Reflection

The mind-body connection is a powerful and intricate relationship between our thoughts, emotions, and physical well-being. This exercise will guide you to explore and strengthen this connection, helping you harness the incredible potential of your mind to positively influence your body. By cultivating awareness and practicing intentional techniques, you can tap into the mind-body connection to enhance your overall health, manage stress, and promote holistic well-being.

Exercise	Duration	Before and After Assessment

Fitness Tracker Challenge

In this interactive table, you can fill out the fitness challenge you want to focus on, set a personal goal, note your starting point, and track your progress over time. Use the "Progress Notes" column to jot down any observations or milestones you achieve, and in the "Strategies and Techniques" column, you can write down any strategies or techniques that help you overcome challenges and make progress towards your goals.

Fitness Challenge	Personal Goal	Starting Point	Techniques	Weekly Progress
Push-ups	30	5	Do 5 more every day	Up to 45!

Reflection Questions

Peak aerobic fitness (VO2 max) has been identified as a crucial indicator of longevity. Delve into your understanding of your body's capabilities. Have you ever considered VO2 max in your fitness goals? How might this knowledge shape your future fitness endeavors?

_____

_____

_____

Reflect on the disparity between the scientifically proven therapeutic benefits of exercise and its often under-emphasized role in healthcare recommendations. How does this disconnect shape your trust in health professionals and influence your approach to personal health responsibility?

_____

_____

_____

The key to longevity is muscle strength, not just mass. Looking at your current fitness routine, how do you prioritize strength over size? What changes can you envisage to better align your routine with this perspective?

_____

_____

_____

Chapter 12: Training 101

The Centenarian Decathlon presents a comprehensive framework that empowers individuals to maintain their current level of fitness well into their later years. This framework revolves around three key pillars: aerobic endurance, muscle strength, and body stability, each crucial for defining and preserving fitness as we age.

Aerobic endurance encompasses a continuum of exercise intensity, ranging from gentle walks to challenging uphill sprints. To optimize overall fitness, it is essential to engage in both steady-state exercises and high-intensity workouts that demand increased oxygen consumption. Aerobic endurance significantly impacts various bodily systems, particularly VO2 max (maximum oxygen consumption) and mitochondrial health.

Muscle loss poses a significant concern, not only for older adults but also for individuals in their 30s, given our contemporary lifestyle. Developing and maintaining muscle strength and power may seem straightforward—lifting heavy weights promotes muscle growth. However, injury prevention is equally crucial. It is vital to exercise caution to avoid injuries that can disrupt progress and result in muscle loss during the recovery phase. Therefore, prioritizing stability training becomes paramount in preventing unnecessary injuries.

By embracing the principles of the Centenarian Decathlon, individuals of all ages can adopt a holistic approach to fitness, focusing on aerobic endurance, muscle strength, and body stability. This proactive approach ensures the preservation of physical fitness and reduces the risk of muscle loss, injury, and age-related decline, enabling individuals to maintain optimal health and vitality throughout their lives.

Key Points

- The calories you burn during exercise are not as important as how you utilize glucose and fatty acids as fuel.

- People with metabolic problems like obesity can't activate their mitochondria to burn fat. Their lack of fitness forces them to rely on glucose as fuel, thus limiting weight loss.

- Active people have greater metabolic flexibility, i.e. they can switch from burning glucose to burning fat with relative ease.

- If you're diabetic, something as simple as a brisk walk for 6 miles a day allows glucose to be sucked out of your bloodstream. This can reduce your dependence on insulin.

- Increasing your VO_2 max as you age can make you as functionally young as someone 12 years your junior.

- Muscle mass declines as you age. However, you lose muscle strength 2-3 times faster than muscle mass. Also, you lose power 2-3 times quicker than you lose muscle strength.

- It's better to start lifting weights while in your younger years. Once sarcopenia sets in, it's very difficult to build muscle mass, no matter how hard you train.

- The human body evolved to carry heavy loads over long distances. Therefore, carrying heavy weights over a distance is critical for maintaining a strong and healthy body.

Fitness Adventure Diary

Imagine yourself on a fitness adventure, exploring new activities and overcoming obstacles related to aerobic endurance, muscle strength, and body stability. Write a diary entry describing a memorable day in this adventure, including the challenges faced, achievements gained, and lessons learned.

_____

_____

_____

_____

_____

_____

_____

_____

_____

_____

_____

_____

_____

_____

_____

_____

_____

Fitness Playlist Creation

Fill in the table with your favorite songs for each category. Consider the energy, tempo, and motivational factors of each song. Select songs that resonate with your workout goals and preferences. Indicate whether the song is suitable for aerobic endurance, muscle strength, or stability exercises. Use this as motivation to curate the perfect playlist for your workouts.

Song Title	Artist	Genre	Activity

Reflection Questions

Reflect on your current aerobic endurance routine. Are you incorporating a balance of steady-state exercises and high-intensity workouts? If not, how can you adjust your routine to optimize your aerobic fitness?

_____

_____

_____

Reflect on your approach to recovery and rest days. How can you ensure that you're giving your body enough time to recover and prevent muscle loss?

_____

_____

_____

Consider your social support system when it comes to fitness. Do you have a network of like-minded individuals who can support and motivate you on your fitness journey? If not, how can you build or expand your support system?

_____

_____

_____

Chapter 13: The Gospel of Stability

Maintaining physical health as we age can be challenging for many individuals, with injuries emerging as the primary obstacle. It is common for people to discontinue their exercise routines after sustaining injuries, leading to a decline in their overall physical well-being.

Injuries should be a significant concern for people of all age groups, even the younger population. While an injury in youth may appear inconsequential at the time, it can have long-term consequences, negatively impacting one's quality of life in the decades to come. Additionally, injuries can also have a psychological impact, further emphasizing the importance of injury prevention for sustained physical fitness throughout life.

To safeguard an active lifestyle and minimize the risk of injuries during exercise, it is crucial to reevaluate how we approach movement. Rather than adhering to the notion of constantly pushing ourselves to the limits during every workout, it is essential to prioritize the development of a solid foundation of stability. By performing exercises with proper form and technique, we enable our bodies to move in alignment with their inherent design.

In essence, adopting a preventive mindset and focusing on building stability can help individuals sustain an active lifestyle throughout their lives. By relearning how to move effectively during exercise and avoiding unnecessary strain, we can minimize the occurrence of injuries and optimize our physical well-being for the long term.

Key Points

- Stability is a measure of how efficiently and safely you can transmit force through your entire body.

- When you lack stability while exercising, the force exerted on your body looks for a way to dissipate. Unfortunately, it often leaks out via the joints, which is why joint injuries are the most common type of exercise injury.

- DNS (dynamic neuromuscular stabilization) is a simple and natural pattern of movements that we relied on when we were infants. However, as we grow up, we somehow lose these healthy, natural patterns of movement.

- The first aspect of stability is breathing. Deep, steady breathing promotes stability and strength while shallow, quick breaths trigger anxiety and increase your risk of injury.

- The ability to stand on one leg has a positive correlation with longevity, especially for people over 50.

- Though personal trainers can teach you how to exercise, don't over-rely on them. At some point, you need to master the different movement patterns on your own.

Proper Movement

This table is intended to serve as a guide for assessing movement alignment. It is important to consult with a qualified fitness professional or healthcare provider for proper instruction and personalized guidance based on your individual needs and limitations. Regularly using this table can help you develop body awareness, improve your movement mechanics, and reduce the risk of injuries. Remember to listen to your body, make necessary adjustments, and seek professional guidance if you have any concerns about your movement alignment.

Exercise	Key Alignment Points	Flaws in Your Posture?

Injury Reflection

Recall a time when you experienced an injury, or injuries, that impacted your physical well-being. Reflect on how it affected your overall health and lifestyle. Write down the specific challenges you faced and the steps you took to recover from the injury, and how it could have been avoided.

_____

_____

_____

_____

_____

_____

_____

_____

_____

_____

_____

_____

_____

_____

_____

_____

_____

_____

_____

Reflection Questions

Other than injuries, what are some of the reasons why people are unable to maintain an active lifestyle in their later years, and how can you avoid them?

_____

_____

_____

Reflect on your physical training journey and contemplate the injuries that have hindered your progress. In what ways have these injuries impacted your ability to reach your full potential? How have they influenced your mindset, motivation, and overall physical well-being?

_____

_____

_____

Reflect on your reliance on personal trainers or fitness professionals. How can you strike a balance between seeking guidance and taking ownership of your own movement patterns and exercises?

_____

_____

_____

Chapter 14: Nutrition 3.0

In today's society, it has become common for individuals to position themselves as health experts, eagerly sharing dietary advice and proclaiming the superiority of their chosen eating regimen. This trend has fostered a religious and tribal atmosphere, with people passionately advocating for their preferred diet while dismissing others' perspectives.

However, upon closer examination, many of these claims lack substantial evidence. The reality is that there is no universally perfect diet that can cater to every individual on Earth. Moreover, the term "diet" itself has been misused and should be replaced with "nutritional biochemistry" to shift the focus towards genuine scientific understanding and eliminate misleading information.

The distinction between a diet and nutritional biochemistry lies in the personalized nature of the latter, which relies on individual feedback and considers factors such as body type and personal goals. Rather than blindly adhering to someone else's dietary rules, the emphasis is on creating a tailored nutrition plan that aligns with one's unique physiology. After all, nobody knows their body better than the individual themselves.

By embracing the concept of nutritional biochemistry and embracing personalized approaches to nourishment, we can move away from unsubstantiated claims and foster a greater understanding of the science behind nutrition. This shift empowers individuals to make informed choices based on their own bodies and goals, promoting a more sensible and effective approach to optimal health.

Key Points

- The food we eat interacts with our genes and microbiome. Since each individual has a unique genome and microbiome, food compounds react differently in each person's body.

- Basic nutritional rules: don't overeat or undereat; consume enough essential fats, protein, minerals, and vitamins; and avoid toxins and pathogens like lead and E. coli.

- Understanding how to interpret nutrition studies is the first step in developing your nutrition plan.

- Epidemiological studies on nutrition are unreliable because they can't distinguish between causation and correlation. They are based on inaccurate data from respondents.

Balanced Plate Design

Create a visual representation of a balanced plate that incorporates the principles of nutritional biochemistry. Divide the plate into appropriate portions for macronutrients, highlight specific foods, and explain the rationale behind your choices. Explain each section of the plate, and why it is important.

Personal Nutritious Manifesto

The personalized nutritious manifesto exercise is a powerful tool for individuals to define their own guiding principles and beliefs when it comes to nutrition and overall health. It allows individuals to reflect on their values, priorities, and goals, and create a personal manifesto that serves as a compass for making informed choices about their diet and lifestyle. Remember, your personalized nutritious manifesto should reflect your unique beliefs and aspirations.

_____

_____

_____

_____

_____

_____

_____

_____

_____

_____

_____

_____

_____

_____

_____

_____

Reflection Questions

Consider your current dietary habits. Are they aligned with your health goals and overall satisfaction? Reflect on why they are or aren't fulfilling, and envisage specific improvements you could implement to enhance your dietary journey.

_____

_____

_____

Contemplate the dual aspects of nutrition and exercise in your wellness journey. Which one, in your personal experience, do you believe has a more profound impact on your health? Delve into the reasons behind your perspective and how it influences your approach to well-being.

_____

_____

_____

Reflect on the multitude of factors influencing your nutritional choices, be it marketing, economics, genetics, religion, peer pressure, or other influences. Which of these holds the most sway for you? Explore why this factor is particularly impactful and how it shapes your dietary decisions.

_____

_____

_____

Chapter 15: Putting Nutritional Biochemistry into Practice

In today's society, it has become increasingly common for individuals to embark on various diets in search of improved health and well-being. Unfortunately, many people find themselves dissatisfied with the outcomes of their chosen dietary approaches. One significant factor contributing to this discontent is the prevalence of the Standard American Diet (SAD). Even when individuals opt to follow a specific diet, they often continue consuming processed foods due to their affordability, widespread availability, appealing taste, and extended shelf life.

However, the consumption of processed foods raises concerns. The issue lies in the excessive intake of low-quality calories from such foods, leading to a deficiency in essential nutrients. The SAD places strain on the body's ability to regulate blood glucose levels and promotes fat storage, thereby disrupting metabolic equilibrium.

In an effort to address this metabolic imbalance, most dietary approaches incorporate three specific strategies:

Caloric restriction: reducing overall food intake to limit calorie consumption

Dietary restriction: eliminating specific foods or food groups from one's diet

Time restriction: adopting specific eating windows or intermittent fasting patterns

While each of these strategies offers its own benefits, it is crucial to recognize their limitations to prevent disappointment and setbacks on the journey to optimal health.

By understanding the drawbacks and advantages associated with these strategies, individuals can make more informed decisions and tailor their approach to suit their unique needs and preferences. This knowledge empowers individuals to navigate their dietary choices more effectively and enhance their overall well-being.

Key Points

- The quality of the food you eat has a greater bearing on your longevity than the quantity of food you consume.

- Caloric restriction may not be necessary if you're already consuming a high-quality diet and are metabolically healthy.

- The biggest benefit of dietary restriction is that you can personalize what you eat. You can even choose the level of restriction of your diet.

- When practicing dietary restriction, don't worry about identifying and eliminating bad foods. Instead, focus on finding the most optimal combination of macronutrients.

- Alcohol has no nutritional value, delays fat oxidation, and often triggers mindless eating.

- Just one night of terrible sleep cripples your ability to metabolize glucose the next day.

- Aerobic exercise reduces blood glucose levels. However, HIIT and resistance training increase glucose temporarily.

- Older people need to consume more protein as they age to avoid losing lean muscle.

- If you exercise, don't eat all your recommended protein serving in a single sitting. Doing so converts amino acids to energy rather than utilizing it for muscle building.

Meal Timing for Muscle Building

Explore the concept of meal timing and its impact on muscle building. Create a meal timing schedule that allows you to consume recommended protein servings throughout the day, optimizing muscle protein synthesis. Note any differences in your energy levels and muscle recovery between different meal timing approaches. In the table, fill in the blanks with the specific time slots for each meal or snack and the corresponding protein serving you plan to consume. This table allows you to organize and visualize your meal timing strategy for muscle building. Adjust the timing and protein servings according to your preferences and schedule.

Meal	Time	Protein Serving	Affects

Quality vs. Quantity

In the table, rate the quality and quantity of each food or meal you consume on a scale of 1 to 10. Consider the nutritional value, freshness, and overall healthiness of the food when determining the quality rating. The quantity rating assesses the portion size or amount of food consumed. Use this table to evaluate and reflect on the balance between quality and quantity in your eating habits. Adjust the ratings based on your personal preferences and goals.

Food/Meal/Snack	Quality (1-10)	Quantity (1-10)	Notes

Reflection Questions

Over-nourishment often manifests as excessive weight gain, frequent feelings of sluggishness or fatigue, and a high likelihood of developing conditions like diabetes or heart disease. Reflecting on these indicators, how would you evaluate your current state of nourishment?

_____

_____

_____

For a metabolically healthy individual, moderate alcohol consumption typically falls within 7 drinks per week for women and 14 for men, according to the Centers for Disease Control and Prevention (as of my last training in September 2021). How does your current alcohol intake align with these guidelines? If necessary, what concrete steps could you take to adjust your alcohol consumption to fall within these healthy limits?

_____

_____

_____

Fasting can be an effective weight loss strategy when practiced responsibly, with methods ranging from intermittent fasting to extended multi-day fasts. Have you ever explored fasting as part of your wellness journey? If so, what type of fasting did you practice, what effects did you experience, and how did this influence your perspective on weight loss and overall health?

_____

_____

_____

Chapter 16: The Awakening

In today's fast-paced society, the prevailing notion suggests that high achievers can thrive on minimal sleep. Sleeping for a full 8 hours is often viewed as a luxury reserved for the idle, while those striving for success must sacrifice sleep to pursue their ambitions. Consequently, many individuals traverse life unaware of the health risks accompanying chronic sleep deprivation.

Research indicates that even a single night of sleep deprivation can induce effects akin to legal intoxication. Insufficient sleep is associated with metabolic dysfunction, hormonal imbalances, impaired memory, depleted energy levels, emotional disturbances, and heightened susceptibility to injuries. The reality is that compromised quantity and quality of sleep can wreak havoc on both your well-being and lifespan.

A restful night's sleep is not exclusive to humans but serves as a vital necessity for all living beings. If sleep held no significance, nature would have phased it out during our evolutionary journey. Moreover, adapting to function on fewer hours of sleep does not equate to it being beneficial for your overall health. Prioritizing and securing adequate sleep will unveil the profound positive impact it can have on various facets of your life.

Key Points

- Severely restricting your sleep raises your insulin resistance by 33 percent. It also makes you irrationally hungry and likely to consume excess calories.

- Poor sleep activates your sympathetic nervous system, thus increasing your cortisol levels, heart rate, and blood pressure. This can trigger a heart attack.

- During deep sleep, your brain cleanses itself of proteins and intercellular junk responsible for neurodegeneration.

- Deep sleep is most important for people between the ages of 40 and 60 to prevent Alzheimer's.

- Though sleep deprivation has negative consequences, oversleeping is not recommended. Sleeping for more than 11 hours is correlated with a higher risk of death.

- Sleep drugs such as Ambien, Valium, and Xanax only induce unconsciousness. They don't encourage deep, healthy sleep and are linked to cognitive decline.

- Laptops, phones, and video games are the worst electronic devices to use before bed. They interfere with sleep quality more than TVs and music players.

- Engaging in endurance exercises during the day can help you fall asleep later at night.

Sleep Quality Assessment

Rate each sleep quality factor on a scale of 1 to 10, with 1 being poor and 10 being excellent. Consider factors such as the duration of sleep, how rested you feel upon waking up, interruptions during sleep, the comfort of your sleep environment, and your overall satisfaction with the quality of sleep. This assessment will help you identify areas for improvement and gain insights into your sleep habits.

Sleep Quality Factors & Notes	Rating (1-10)
Duration (hours):	
Restfulness Upon Waking:	
Sleep Interruptions:	
Sleep Environment:	
Overall Satisfaction:	
Most Notable Factors:	

Sleep Environment Makeover

Use the Sleep Environment Makeover table provided below to evaluate different factors that can impact your sleep quality. Rate each factor on a scale of 1 to 5, with 1 being poor and 5 being excellent. Consider the lighting conditions in your bedroom, the level of noise present, the temperature of the room, and the comfort and quality of your bedding. Be honest with your assessment to identify areas that need improvement.

Sleep Environment Factors	Assessment (1-5)	Improvement Ideas
Lighting		
Noise		
Temperature		
Bedding		

Reflection Questions

Reflect on the number of hours of quality sleep you generally obtain each night. How does this measure up against the often-recommended 7-9 hours? Evaluate whether you find this quantity adequate for maintaining your energy levels and mental clarity throughout the day, and why.

_____

_____

_____

Rate your ease of falling asleep within 30 minutes of going to bed on a scale of 1 (very easy) to 10 (extremely difficult). If you face challenges, what factors might be causing this difficulty? Consider specific strategies you could implement to facilitate a smoother transition into sleep.

_____

_____

_____

Consider the frequency of occasions when you wake up during the night and struggle to return to sleep. What could be the potential triggers for these disruptions? Contemplate on practical changes you could make in your pre-sleep routine or sleep environment to minimize these nocturnal awakenings.

_____

_____

_____

Chapter 17: Work in Progress

In discussions surrounding longevity and healthspan, our attention is predominantly directed towards physical well-being. Mainstream medicine emphasizes the significance of medications, and to some extent, diet and exercise. However, the often-neglected aspect of emotional health holds equal importance in this discourse. Society's failure to prioritize emotional well-being is responsible for the surge in suicides, overdoses, addictions, and self-destructive behaviors that we witness today.

Emotional health must form an integral part of any endeavor to enhance longevity. After all, why would one aspire to lead a long and healthy life if it is marred by misery and a sense of unfulfillment? Unresolved emotional trauma often drives individuals towards self-medication with drugs and alcohol. For many, this pattern becomes a form of "slow-motion suicide," as they prefer a gradual self-destruction rather than confronting their deep-seated traumas.

Trauma takes on various manifestations, and adapting to one's anger or addiction does not signify an absence of underlying issues. It is crucial to acknowledge and identify the root causes of emotional struggles to pave the way for the necessary assistance and healing one requires.

Key Points

- There are 5 classes of trauma: abuse, neglect, abandonment, enmeshment, and witnessing tragic events.

- A major terrible event can be traumatizing. But multiple little traumas (e.g. living with an alcoholic parent) can be just as damaging yet more difficult to confront.

- Failure to adapt to trauma leads to addiction, codependency, attachment disorders, and survival strategies.

- The most difficult part of dealing with emotional health is your inability to identify the need to make a change. Most people don't realize that they need help with their trauma.

- Instead of worrying about resume virtues (i.e. professional accomplishments), focus more on your eulogy virtues (i.e. what your loved ones will say about you when you die).

- The only true remedy for healing emotional wounds is self-exploration. This is an uncomfortable process that takes time and daily action.

Emotional Inventory

Emotions play a powerful role in our lives, influencing our thoughts, actions, and overall well-being. However, sometimes it can be challenging to understand and navigate our emotions effectively. This exercise is designed to help you gain insight into your emotional landscape by identifying common emotions, their triggers, and healthy coping mechanisms.

Emotion	Trigger	Coping Mechanism

Trauma Reflection

This exercise will help you explore and understand the traumas you have experienced, identify their effects, and initiate the healing process. By engaging in this reflection, you can gain insights into how trauma has shaped your life and begin the journey of compassionate self-exploration. Take this courageous step towards acknowledging and addressing your wounds, fostering resilience, and reclaiming your power.

Trauma	Effects/Reaction	Coping Mechanisms	Healing Strategies

Life Values Assessment

Understanding our core values is essential for living a purposeful and fulfilling life. Our values shape our decisions, actions, and priorities, guiding us towards what truly matters to us. However, in the midst of our busy lives, it's easy to lose sight of our values or become disconnected from them. The Life Values Assessment is a powerful tool that helps us identify and clarify our most important values, allowing us to align our choices and goals with what is truly meaningful to us. By exploring and honoring our values, we can make conscious decisions that lead to greater fulfillment, happiness, and authenticity.

Life Domain	Core Values and Beliefs	Notes

Reflection Questions

Reflect on instances when you may have supported a loved one through their trauma. How did you contribute to their healing process, and what lessons did you glean from this experience? Could these insights be applicable to managing your own life's challenges?

_____

_____

_____

Consider the impact of any traumatic experiences from your childhood on your personal development. Do you perceive these experiences as having made you stronger or weaker? Delve into the ways these experiences have shaped your resilience, vulnerability, and overall character.

_____

_____

_____

Undertake an exploration of your family lineage. Can you pinpoint any generational trauma that seems to have been passed down through the years? Identify the ways this inherited trauma might have influenced your life, and ponder on potential strategies to heal and break the cycle for future generations.

_____

_____

_____

About the Author

Dr. Peter Attia is an author, surgeon, and podcaster. He received his medical degree from Stanford University and trained as a surgeon for 5 years at the John Hopkins Hospital. He then spent 2 years as a surgical oncology fellow at the National Institutes of Health, where he focused on immune-based therapies for melanoma. He is also the founder of *Early Medical*, a medical practice created to improve lifespan and healthspan using the principles of Medicine 3.0. He hosts *The Drive*, a podcast that covers health and medicine issues. Dr. Attia lives in Texas with his family.

Thank you!

Companion Press is a collective of students, writers, editors, designers, and researchers that focus on bringing you the best companion workbooks on Amazon.

We would like to thank you for helping us support our passions. We hope you learned new and exciting information from this book that will carry on into your daily life.

If you enjoyed this workbook, would you please leave us a five-star review? This will allow us to continue to produce high-quality workbooks based on your favorite best-sellers.

Scan the QR code below and
leave your review now!

Made in the USA
Las Vegas, NV
19 August 2023

76272745R00059